Original title:
Tales from the Tropics

Copyright © 2025 Creative Arts Management OÜ
All rights reserved.

Author: Levi Montgomery
ISBN HARDBACK: 978-1-80581-741-3
ISBN PAPERBACK: 978-1-80581-268-5
ISBN EBOOK: 978-1-80581-741-3

Whispers of the Caribbean Breeze

A parrot's gossip fills the air,
With tales of coconuts that dare.
The crabs in suits, they strut with glee,
Claiming they own the sandy spree.

Cocktails spill in laughter's grace,
As iguanas win the dance-off race.
The sun slips down with a wink so sly,
While seagulls plot to catch the fry.

Secrets Beneath the Canopy

Lizards play poker in the shade,
While monkeys swing with a grand parade.
A toucan's laugh, a wild delight,
Turns evening into a comical flight.

Under palms, there's a party vibe,
With turtles sharing their best jive.
While frogs croak jokes in ribbit tones,
The night comes alive with silly tones.

Echoes of Island Legends

A fisherman tells tales so bizarre,
Of mermaids caught in a salsa bar.
The wind carries giggles from the sea,
As fish swap stories of wild jubilee.

Legends that tickle the island ears,
Of crabs that toast to forgotten years.
The moon chuckles, a gleeful night,
As coconuts rumble with pure delight.

The Lullaby of Palm Trees

Palm trees sway with a cheeky grin,
As beach balls bounce with a playful spin.
A hammock sings to the passing breeze,
While laughter echoes through the tall leaves.

A shrimp in shades jokes with a crab,
Making the sun a little drab.
As sunset paints a colorful cheer,
The island whispers, "Come join here!"

Sagas of Swaying Silhouettes

In the shadows of a palm, we dance,
A crab scuttles by, in a clumsy prance.
The sun's a jester, with its bright glare,
While locals laugh, tossing worries to air.

Monkeys swing high, with bananas in hand,
They drop their fruit as they make their stand.
A parrot squawks jokes, its colors so bright,
As the whole beach joins in, what a sight!

Oceanic Odes from the Isle

The waves tell tales of a ship made of foam,
With fish in tuxedos, calling it home.
Crabs hold a reunion, in shells they reside,
While sea turtles surf, with laughter as their guide.

Seagulls report, on the sand they decree,
That sunbathers snore, a sight to see.
As dolphins perform, flipping high with glee,
Each splash of their tails is a wild jubilee!

The Charm of Coconut Candles

Coconuts glow on a warm tropical night,
Casting soft beams, what a delightful sight!
The crickets all chirp, in a rhythmic delight,
As the iguanas sway, in the shimmering light.

A coconut fell, rolling down a hill,
Chasing after the laughter, the thrill of the chill.
While we sip from piña coladas galore,
And dance 'til we drop, calling for more!

Flavors of the Tropical Spirit

Mangoes are laughing, ripe on the tree,
While pineapples twirl, singing so free.
With each zesty bite, the joy is revealed,
As everyone shares what the tropics have healed.

A party of fruits, in a colorful bowl,
Guava plays tambourine, as passion fruit strolls.
The rhythm of flavors, wild and sweet,
Ends with laughter, who could ask for more heat?

Narratives in Nautical Night

Under the stars, the sailors sing,
Fish in the ocean wear a bling.
A crab in a hat, quite the sight,
Dancing along, oh what a night!

A dolphin jokes, 'What's your quest?'
The anchor replies, 'Just taking a rest!'
A parrot laughs, with a wink so sly,
'You're moored in the best of the sky!'

The Spirit of the Sea Turtle

A turtle in shades, gliding with grace,
Carrying wisdom, in a slow-paced race.
'Young ones, oh listen,' he says with a grin,
'Life's not a rush, let the fun begin!'

A wave rolls up, and the turtle does sway,
While crabs clamor close, trying to play.
'Keep calm and chill, enjoy what you see,'
He chuckles aloud, 'Let's just be free!'

Rippling Reflections of the Tropic Sky

The sun dips low, a big orange ball,
Fish jump around, trying not to fall.
A pelican swoops, steals a snack,
While a goat on the shore plans its next hack.

The clouds paint smiles, silly and bright,
As a monkey throws coconuts in flight.
The breezy giggles, well they never cease,
In the land of warm laughs, there's always peace!

Insights from Island Inhabitants

In a huddle of huts, the people conspire,
Over grilled fish and a spark of fire.
A cat tells tales, with a swish and a purr,
'You humans talk too much, just watch and stir!'

A parrot bickers with the gossipy breeze,
'Who's the silliest of us? It's such a tease!'
With laughter that dances on the waves' embrace,
The island's spirit lights up the place.

Petals of the Passionflower

A butterfly danced on a hot summer day,
Wearing a hat made of bright lemonade.
The flowers all giggled, they swayed in delight,
As bees buzzed around, buzzing jokes out of sight.

The parrot cracked jokes, his feathers so bright,
Telling tales of the fruit that was comically ripe.
The mangoes turned red, they burst out in cheer,
Whispering, "We're juicy, let's party right here!"

Adventures Under the Golden Sun

In a hammock that swung, two coconuts lounged,
Playing checkers with crabs who were quite astound.
The sun beamed down like a golden big grin,
While palm trees waved flags of a tropical win.

A lizard in shades shared some jokes with the breeze,
Claiming he'd found the world's biggest cheese!
But the cheese was just moonlight, all shiny and grand,
Everyone laughed as it slipped through the sand.

Breeze-Whispered Secrets

The breeze told a secret to a very wise owl,
Who hooted in answer with a chuckle and howl.
"What's round, soft, and fluffy? A cloud in disguise!
I've seen it float by, with a wink in its eyes!"

The trees leaned in closer, their leaves in a whirl,
As the shy flowers giggled, giving a twirl.
They whispered of coconuts falling from trees,
And the laughter that echoed on sweet, playful seas.

The Colorful Canvas of Paradise

The sky wore crayons, a vibrant display,
With turtles in top hats, leading the way.
They painted the ocean with splashes of fun,
While dolphins played tag in the shimmering sun.

The sand looked like cake, and the waves flew a kite,
As goofy sea creatures danced through the night.
A jellyfish juggled, a clam clapped along,
In this land of delights, it all felt so wrong!

Hushed Whispers of the Wild

In a jungle filled with chatter,
Monkeys plot, their plans a clatter.
A parrot mimics with great flair,
Saying, "What's for lunch? I don't care!"

Lizards bask on rocks so warm,
While ants march by in perfect swarm.
A sloth yawns wide, then starts to sneeze,
Sending leaves down like fallen leaves.

A toucan laughs, its beak so bright,
"Let's play hide and seek tonight!"
But before the game could start their fun,
The sun slipped down, and day was done.

In this giggling green parade,
Spines mean nothing, fears allayed.
For in the wild, so wily and free,
Nature's humor is wild—and so are we!

Footprints in the Sand

On a beach where seabirds prance,
Sandy toes take a clumsy chance.
A crab snaps back with sassy glee,
"Watch your step! You're scaring me!"

The waves roll in, then roll on out,
With each rush, there's laughter and shout.
A toddler tumbles, sand in hair,
As a dolphin leaps to steal the glare.

Shells scatter, like confetti thrown,
And the sun shines down on skin well-grown.
"Are we swimming yet?" someone did say,
As the tide pulls back to start the play.

Footprints mix in joy and mess,
Creating maps of our little stress.
Yet under the sun, bright and grand,
We write our stories in this golden sand!

A Symphony of Tropical Heartbeats

In a grove where laughter churns,
Coconut trees sway, secrets stir.
"Who stole my drink?" a monkey shrieks,
As toucans gossip in colorful peaks.

The beat of drums from the night parade,
Echo softly, their rhythms played.
An iguana groove, with style and sway,
Teaches all the other critters his way.

With maracas made of seeds and shells,
Crickets chirp their own jolly jells.
"Let's dance!" cries out a colorful frog,
In this symphony of bliss and a bog.

Nature's band, we all partake,
Even the night owls start to shake.
In the tropics, laughter's the key,
To a heart that beats wild and free!

Reflections on the Aqua Horizon

As the sun dips low, hues collide,
In the water, all fears subside.
A shrimp goes by with a strut so proud,
Waving, "Look at me!" to the fishy crowd.

The waves giggle, whispering tales,
Of flamboyant fish and their glittery scales.
"Dance a little, join in the fun,"
Their splashes shout, "Let's soak in the sun!"

Beneath the surface, shark jokes swirl,
While clowns in sea anemones twirl.
"Is that a wave, or just your hair?"
"Let's catch some laughs, float without care!"

This aqua world, a vast delight,
Reflections shine with colors bright.
And as we swim in this salty spree,
Mother Ocean holds a joke just for me!

Raindrops on the Lotus Leaf

Raindrops dance like tiny clowns,
Bouncing on leaves in fruit-filled towns.
Frogs in tuxedos take a leap,
Singing loud, they wake from sleep.

A lizard slides with cheeky flair,
Winks at the world without a care.
Butterflies, they twirl and glide,
In this joyful, splashy ride.

The lotus chuckles, sways with glee,
As droplets espy, 'Oh look at me!'
While fish below with fishy jokes,
Giggle and tease a pond of blokes.

Under the sun, the fun won't end,
Where nature plays, and laughter bends.
Every raindrop, a whimsical tale,
In the tropical sun, we sail and sail.

Tide Pools and Treasures

In tide pools filled with jelly beans,
Crabs in disco dance routines.
Starfish sporting glittering shoes,
Chart their moves like ocean blues.

A sea snail crawls with stars in tow,
Singing songs of the ebb and flow.
While fishes giggle, winking bright,
In these puddles, what a sight!

Shelf upon shelf of ocean's loot,
An octopus dons a treasure suit.
Pearls and shells, a fashion parade,
Strutting around, not the least bit frayed.

"Can you believe this?" whispers the coral,
"This party's better than anything mortal!"
Waves crash with laughter, time runs free,
Tide pools holding joy just for me.

Whispers of the Waving Palms

Palms gossip like tickled friends,
Their leaves a-buzz with fun amends.
They sway and shimmy, giggle loud,
Enticing the breeze, they form a crowd.

Coconuts roll with silly spins,
Chasing each other, everyone wins!
A parrot mimics a laugh or two,
Adding to the chatter, it feels brand new.

Swaying to rhythms of chummy beats,
Palm trees share their goofiest tweets.
Underneath, the sand grins wide,
As this tropical humor cannot hide.

In the sky, where laughter leans,
Nature's humor swirls in greens.
With whispers soft, the palm leaves tease,
In this funny tropical breeze.

Shadows Beneath Swaying Trees

Beneath the trees where shadows play,
Squirrels hold a nutty buffet.
Their chatter echoes in the air,
As they feast without a care.

A monkey swings with silly flair,
Stealing snacks from those unaware.
Coconuts tumble, what a scene,
Nature's laughter, oh so keen!

The shadows stretch like loungers free,
Inviting all to join the spree.
Creatures whisper jokes and cheer,
In this leafy world, there's nothing to fear.

As sunbeams peak, a lively show,
Nature's circus begins to glow.
Under swaying branches, we all agree,
Life's a giggle beneath these trees.

Glimpses of Glistening Coasts

The palm trees swayed in a silly dance,
While crabs donned hats and took a chance.
A parrot squawked a tune so sweet,
It made the fishermen tap their feet.

The waves rolled in, a giggling tease,
Surfboards chased the bumblebees.
Seashells whispered jokes to the shore,
As sunbathers laughed and shouted for more.

A dolphin flipped, a playful dive,
While tourists snapped photos, feeling alive.
With sandy toes and sun-kissed skin,
This coastal life where smiles begin.

Harmonious Hues of Dusk

The sky wore a coat of pastel delight,
As the sun waved goodbye, taking flight.
A goat on a hill dressed in shades of pink,
Managed a wink as the crickets did wink.

Fireflies twinkled, a parade of lights,
While frogs croaked out their funny insights.
A monkey swung down, stole the show,
And shared its banana with a friendly crow.

Stars began to twinkle, looking bemused,
As night took over, everyone amused.
Laughter echoed through the vibrant leaves,
In this magic moment, the world believes.

Sunset Stories of Solitude

Alone on the beach, with a book in hand,
A seagull squawked, planning a band.
The sun dipped low, with a wink of gold,
While a beach ball plotted to be bold.

A cat on a surfboard, oh what a sight,
Trying to catch waves with sheer delight.
It fell with a splash, and let out a yowl,
As fish swam past, bursting in howl.

The ocean chuckled, a playful tease,
As the sun painted portraits with the breeze.
Stories unfolded, in the twilight's glow,
Where solitude mingled, and laughter flowed.

Garden of the Gifted Winds

In a garden where flowers sprouted in cheer,
A breeze whispered secrets, oh so near.
The daisies giggled, their heads held high,
While tulips curtsied, reaching for the sky.

A hedgehog painted rainbows with glee,
Chasing butterflies, wild and free.
Grasshoppers dressed in dapper attire,
Danced on the petals, never to tire.

The sun threw confetti, splashes of light,
As pollen performed in a dazzling flight.
In this garden of laughter, all things collide,
With humorous blooms, in joy, they abide.

Embraces of the Ocean Horizon

The waves dance like a jig, oh so light,
A seagull swoops in, what a sight!
It snatches my fries with a cheeky grin,
Who knew lunch would spark such a din?

A crab in a tux, dashing and bold,
Tries to impress, or so I'm told.
He sidesteps my toes, oh the glee!
A promenade of crabs, fancy and free!

The sunset spills colors, a paint palette wide,
Fish flash by like glitter, zipping with pride.
I laugh at the ocean's silly parade,
Even the dolphins seem slightly dismayed!

As nightfall approaches, the stars start to wink,
The ocean begins its jubilant sync.
In this embrace of the vast ocean blue,
I can't help but giggle — what a view!

The Symphony of Rainy Seasons

Raindrops tap dance on the roof, oh so grand,
Creating a tune that makes us all stand.
Umbrellas flip-flop, a colorful mess,
As puddles bloom with laughs, I confess!

The sky's a canvas, grey and bold,
A parrot in raincoat, or so I'm told!
He squawks at the clouds, entire brigade,
While critters prepare for a playful parade!

A frog plops down, in a most regal way,
Decides it's time for a leap and a sway.
His splash sends ripples—a water ballet,
I chuckle at nature's lively display!

With thunderous snaps and lightning's bright flash,
Each moment's a giggle, a thunderous clash.
The rainy season sings a sweet, silly song,
Where laughter and raindrops merrily belong!

Rediscovering the Wild Tropics

In the jungle, where the wild things roam,
A monkey in glasses claims it as home.
Swinging from vines with impeccable flair,
I think, does he care for my picnic fare?

A toucan pops by, colors like fire,
Challenging me to a fruit-eating choir.
We munch on bananas, a slimy affair,
And giggles erupt in the humid air.

A sloth takes its time to cross the path,
With so much to do, it just makes me laugh!
It waves as it passes, all slow and grand,
I stop to applaud this impressive stand.

The tropics are wild, yet filled with delight,
Each creature a wonder, each day a new sight.
From dancing to munching, a whimsical spree,
In this verdant realm, I feel so carefree!

Starlit Stories Above the Bay

Under a sky twinkling like confetti,
A crab in a top hat looks quite ready.
He tells tales of seas and bright, shiny loot,
With a comedic flair that's utterly cute!

Stars above twinkle in glee, it seems,
As fish form a chorus, joining our dreams.
The moon rolls its eyes at crabby old tales,
While fireflies dance like tiny fair sails.

A night bird croons love songs of the deep,
While dolphins whirl by in a giggling leap.
With sea breezes laughing, oh what a night,
As waves hum along, everything feels right!

So here we gather, under starlit glow,
In a wacky world where silly things flow.
With each glance up, laughter fills the bay,
As stories unfold, bright and briskly gay!

Lullabies of the Coconut Grove

Under palm trees, monkeys swing,
Coconuts drop, oh what a sting!
Parrots squawk a silly tune,
While crabs dance beneath the moon.

A frog croaks loud, a lizard scoffs,
The sunburned tourists drop their scoffs.
With coconut drinks in hand they sway,
And laugh till night turns into day.

A bear-sized rat steals a fruity pie,
While sleepy sloths just roll on by.
The breeze comically plays its part,
As beach balls bounce with a merry heart.

In this grove, all's light and bright,
Even the night has a funny bite.
With giggles in the air's embrace,
Lullabies bring a smile to each face.

The Heartbeat of Hidden Havens

In a hammock, a parrot preens,
Humming tunes of tropical dreams.
A turtle coughs in an awkward fit,
While crabs join in, making it a skit.

Underwater, fish boast their colors,
While seabirds roll their eyes at others.
An octopus tells tales so wild,
Even the seashells can't help but smiled.

Sunsets bring a playful glow,
Fishermen's nets get caught in tow.
With laughter echoing from the bay,
Every heartbeat finds a way to play.

Hidden havens, secrets unfold,
Where life's a dance, bright and bold.
With every wave, a chuckle flows,
As nature's whimsy ever grows.

Symphonies of the Tropical Night

Cicadas sing in rhythmic cheer,
While fireflies buzz, drawing near.
A raccoon sneaks a curious stroll,
Stealing fruit as if on a roll.

Bats dip low in a comical swoop,
Dodging the frogs in their nightly loop.
The moonlight winks, a playful tease,
And rustling leaves dance in the breeze.

Tropical breezes hum a tune,
As raccoons plot 'neath the silver moon.
Each little critter plays its part,
In this symphony of joy and art.

Through the darkness, laughter rings,
Nature holds court, and everyone sings.
With smiles shared on this magical flight,
Life's a jolly dance, such a delight!

Mysteries of Mangrove Roots

In muddy waters where secrets dwell,
Mangroves whisper, 'Can you tell?'
A crab gives wink, a prankster bright,
As fish flip for comedic delight.

Wiggly worms gather for a show,
With mangrove trees as their front row.
An otter slips with a splashing cheer,
In waters tangled, laughter draws near.

Branches twist in a curious way,
Home to creatures who love to play.
With each twist and turn, they plot their schemes,
Finding fun in the wildest dreams.

Oh, the mysteries lurking here,
Beneath the roots, good vibes appear.
Nature's comedy, wild and free,
A joyful dance, just wait and see!

Sunlit Stories of the Shore

A crab wore glasses, thought he was suave,
Strutting on the sand like he owned the wave.
Seagulls laughed at his dapper style,
He winked back, flaunting his own toothy smile.

A dolphin in flip-flops danced with a flair,
Trying to impress a turtle named Claire.
They tripped on seaweed, oh what a sight,
Rolled in the surf, in pure delight.

A sunburned octopus with sunblock in hand,
Fell asleep on the shore, oh, wasn't it grand?
Woke up all splotchy, looking quite daft,
His friends burst out laughing, couldn't hold their craft.

The tide brought whispers of coconut jokes,
While crabs held a meeting with curious folks.
"Why did the fish go to school?" they all cheered,
"To catch up on lessons, it's quite clear!"

Dance of the Hibiscus

A flower in tutu twirled in the breeze,
Catching the stares of the busy honeybees.
She strutted and swayed, quite sure of her moves,
While butterflies giggled in silky grooves.

A parrot in shades gave commentary loud,
"Look at that bloom, isn't she proud?"
The hibiscus just blushed, as bright as a flame,
"Keep flapping your beak, I'm winning this game!"

When the sun set low, a dance-off began,
Even the palm trees swayed to the plan.
With coconuts clapping, the rhythm was right,
Nature's own party, a glorious sight.

The night wore a crown of stars shining bright,
Each petal kept twirling till the dawn's light.
They all laughed together at the joy they had shared,
In the dance of the flowers, none ever despaired.

Shadows of the Mangrove Mysteries

In shadows of roots where the sneaky crabs play,
Lurking in mud, they chase their own prey.
A monkey dropped bananas, oh what a blunder,
It echoed through branches, a thunderous wonder.

A wise old heron, with one eye quite sly,
Cackled at antics from the branches nearby.
"Why did you cross the stream?" he did tease,
"To get to the other side, if you please!"

Raccoons in masks plotted their next scheme,
To swipe all the fruits from the jungle's sweet dream.
They giggled and snickered, not quite discreet,
The wind gave a chuckle, a mischievous beat.

But the stingray laughed loud from beneath the waves,
"Stop your frolicking, you silly knaves!
There's treasure afoot, with sand dollars aglow,
Let's venture together and see what we know."

Serenade of the Sapphire Sea

The waves sang a tune with a splash and a flip,
While fish held a concert on a coral cliff.
"They say we're fin-tastic," one trumpet fish crooned,
As sea turtles swayed, completely marooned.

A starfish, quite shy, tried to join in the fun,
But tangled in kelp, he forgot how to run.
The laughter erupted, echoing free,
In the laughter of bubbles, enchanted sea.

A whale with a hat joined the ribbiting crew,
Singing baritone twangs, a whale's dream debut.
The dolphins danced wildly, creating a scene,
"Who knew the ocean had such rhythm and sheen?"

Under the moonlight, the sea sparkled bright,
While the sand crabs tapped to the music's delight.
With smiles and jokes, the night filled with glee,
In the serenade vast of the sapphire sea.

Serenade of the Sunset Beach

A crab with a hat, oh what a sight,
Sipping on juice, feeling just right.
His friends on the shore, they start to cheer,
Dancing with waves, they're all full of beer.

The sun waves goodbye with a wink and a grin,
As the seagulls gather and join in the spin.
They squawk and they flap, like they own the place,
A party of feathers, with rhythm and grace.

The lighthouse keeps watch with a twinkling eye,
While starfish tell stories and jellyfish fly.
Oh, what a spectacle, laughter rings free,
On this wild coastline, just you and me.

As night spills its colors, the moon strikes a pose,
The beach starts to sparkle, just like your nose.
With flip-flops and fun, we dance without care,
At the serenade hour, we're one with the air.

The Dance of Lush Rainforests

In the thicket of green, where the toucans chatter,
Frogs wear top hats, it's a real fun platter.
They leap and they croak, like they're on a show,
Each jump is a jig, in the mud they go.

Vines swing in rhythm, like a grand ballet,
Monkeys start swirling, in their own crazy way.
With banana confetti raining from the sky,
The tree trunks all shimmy, and the beetles fly.

A sloth dressed in bowtie sways slow like a breeze,
While ants hold a picnic with crumbs and some cheese.
The parrots on drums, keeping beats that are wild,
In this jungle disco, we're all like a child.

When evening arrives, the fireflies fumble,
With winks and with giggles, the whole forest tumbles.
Such mirth in the leaves, it echoes alive,
In the dance of the lush, the spirits arrive.

Secrets of the Sapphire Sea

Beneath the blue waves, where the fish wear suits,
Octopuses gossip, exchanging their roots.
The dolphins are diving, with flips that amuse,
In a world full of laughter, there's no time to snooze.

Sea turtles in shades lounge under the sun,
Sipping on cocktails, oh, don't they have fun!
They've got stories to tell, but they're slow as can be,
It's a race through the surf, will you keep up with me?

The coral reefs dance, with colors so bright,
A party of krill twirls, oh what a sight!
They shimmy and glide, with confetti of foam,
In the secrets they share, we all feel at home.

As dusk meets the sea, with giggles and glee,
Stars twinkle above in a watery spree.
With laughter like waves, and joy in each spray,
The sapphire sea whispers, swim here and play!

Echoes of the Island Breeze

On the shore where the palms sway, a breeze starts to tease,
It tickles the tourists, makes them feel free.
A parrot named Charlie, with jokes up his wing,
Sings songs of the island, oh, what fun they bring!

The sandcastles crumble, with waves that betray,
But the kids just erupt into laughter and play.
They splash in the water, they grin and they leap,
While mermaids giggle, their secrets they keep.

As the sun sets low, bringing colors so bold,
The breeze tells a story, a tale to be told.
With coconuts rolling and laughter so sweet,
Every moment is magic, as life skips a beat.

Echoes of joy, through the air they resound,
In this vibrant paradise, happiness found.
With breezes that dance and laughter at ease,
We savor the flavors, all thanks to the breeze.

Enchanted Rainforest Reveries

In the jungle, monkeys swing,
Telling jokes like it's a fling.
Parrots squawk with laughs so bright,
While sloths take naps, the day turns night.

Frogs in fancy hats, oh my!
Leap in rhythm, almost fly.
Caterpillars dance on leaves so green,
A party scene you've never seen.

Lemurs juggling fruits so ripe,
While lizards offer some fresh hype.
The forest floor's a dance-off floor,
Nature's humor, who could ask for more?

Coconut shells used as drums,
As elephant friends come and hum.
In laughter's arms, they all unite,
These jungle gems, a pure delight.

The Spirit of the Coconut Grove

In the grove where coconuts fall,
A palm tree whispers, 'Listen all!'
Crabs wearing sandals, what a sight,
Tap dance together, day and night.

Underneath the swaying fronds,
Laughter echoes; life responds.
Turtles twerking on the sand,
Bringing joy, oh so grand!

A silly parrot, with a wink,
Sips on nectar, starts to think.
'Why walk when you can shimmy fast?'
Coconut parties that will last!

Surfboards made of leafy greens,
Waves that roll beneath the scenes.
With each splash, a chuckle flows,
In coconut land, anything goes!

Lost in the Lush

In the heart of green, I roam astray,
Tangled vines lead me on my way.
The squirrels giggle as I trip,
I swear I'll find another grip!

Beetles marching in a line,
Parade of bugs, oh how divine!
Butterflies think they hold the crown,
While frogs startle with a bound.

A snake in shades, slick as can be,
Slides past me, grinning with glee.
"Lost, are you? Here, take a hint!"
I laugh so hard, can't catch my breath!

But then a vine wraps round my shoe,
And pulls me back, a comedic cue.
Maybe lost isn't so bad,
In this lush world, I'm still glad!

Fables of the Coral Reef

Under waves, the fish convene,
Sharing stories, quite the scene.
A clownfish slips with a joke so witty,
"A starfish left me for the city!"

Sea turtles laugh at jellyfishes' prance,
With every wiggle, it seems to dance.
Blowfish puffing up in pride,
While shrimp unite, side by side.

The octopus pulls pranks galore,
Ink clouds hide, then they explore.
Corals giggle in colors bright,
Setting the sea alive with light.

But then a diver thinks he's the king,
With bubbles rising, we start to sing.
In underwater chuckles, life is brave,
In this coral world, we all misbehave!

Moonlit Nights in Paradise

In the palm trees, shadows dance,
Under stars, we take a chance.
A coconut falls with a comical thud,
We laugh aloud, it's just a dud.

The crabs in tuxedos scuttle quick,
Dodging waves like a party trick.
Swaying to rhythms, they lose their grip,
And tumble down, oh what a trip!

Fireflies twinkle, a disco show,
They flash like they've had too much to glow.
We sip on cocktails, slippery and bright,
Cheers to the night that feels so right!

The moon, a spotlight on this scene,
It giggles soft, a silver sheen.
In paradise, nights are full of cheer,
With laughter loud, let's raise a beer!

The Heartbeat of the Jungle

A toucan tells a joke so grand,
His colorful beak, a helping hand.
Swinging monkeys with their savvy style,
Make us laugh, it's been a while.

The jaguar slips, lose a paw,
Then hits the leaves with a comical flaw.
A parrot squawks, "What's the deal?"
In this heartbeat, joy is real.

Bamboo bends with a giggly creak,
As the sloths go by, moving at peak.
A dance-off breaks out on the ground,
With moves so wild, we spin around!

Beneath the trees where mishaps loom,
Nature's humor makes the flowers bloom.
In this jungle, laughter holds the key,
To find the joy in life's uproarious spree!

Where the Conch Shell Speaks

A conch shell whispers tales at dawn,
"Listen close, don't yawn!"
With every buzz, it spins its yarn,
Of fish in suits, oh what a charm!

The waves giggle as they play at shore,
Singing songs of an ocean encore.
A fish wearing glasses swims by with flair,
Adjusts them carefully, "I'm almost there!"

The beach crabs form a marching band,
With tiny cymbals in the sand.
As seagulls squawk, what a sound,
In the laughter of waves, joy abounds.

In seashells' echo, dreams arise,
With silly sparkles and goofy skies.
Listen closely, let giggles unfurl,
In the shell's voice, explore the world!

Dreamscapes of the Island Goddess

In dreams, she dances on the sea,
With flips and twirls, wild and free.
Her laughter rings like coconut bells,
Echoing through the jungle swells.

Palm trees join in the whimsical cheer,
Shaking fronds, they clap, my dear.
A boisterous breeze whispers her name,
The island's heart beats with a playful fame.

Moonbeams paint the sand so bright,
As starfish giggle in pure delight.
She weaves her magic in the night air,
With sparkles of mischief dancing everywhere.

Here, dreams are woven with silly thread,
Making us chuckle from toe to head.
An island goddess, with a cheeky grin,
In every heart, the fun begins!

Enchanted Evenings by the Shoreline

The sun dips low, a golden fry,
Seagulls laugh as they swoop by.
A crab in sunglasses starts to dance,
While tourists take a silly stance.

Laughter bubbles like the waves,
Tanned folks tripping over knaves.
A parrot chats, then echoes loud,
'Why's everyone acting so cowed?'

Drinks in hand, they spill and spill,
As ocean breezes play their thrill.
A flip-flop flies, a wife does shout,
'Who needs this? Let's head out!'

But nighttime brings a wobbly moon,
Fishes flip, and mermaids croon.
Under stars, they chuckle tight,
'Next year, let's not choose a flight!'

The Lure of the Tropical Isle

Palm trees sway, a breezy call,
What's that behind the waterfall?
A monkey's head pops out with glee,
Grabbing snacks from the family tree.

Kids build castles in the sand,
As a stray dog becomes the band.
He howls along with a coconut,
'The best beach party is this nut!'

Coconut drinks with tiny straws,
Drunk flamingos wrestling for applause.
A lizard struts in sunken clothes,
Claiming he could win the pose.

But locals grin, they know the score,
At sunset, laughter stirs the shore.
With every splash, their worries flee,
Island life is wild and free!

Moments in the Moonlit Lagoon

Under the glow of the silver night,
Frog choruses join the starlit flight.
A turtle glides; he has a dream,
To win a race or join the stream.

Fireflies flicker like tiny stars,
While fish tell tales of strange bazars.
A hippo hums a silly tune,
'This place feels like a cartoon!'

Drunken crickets take to the stage,
While toads lament the turning page.
With every ribbit, the laughter grows,
As beachgoers dispute their woes.

Snapshot moments that make them cheer,
'Next time, let's bring the giraffe here!'
With giggles bright under the gleam,
They dance as if it's all a dream.

Harmonies of the Hummingbird Flight

In blossoms where the sun does zoom,
Hummingbirds buzz, causing a boom.
One fluffs feathers, strikes a pose,
Shaking its tail to woo a rose.

'You dance too fast!' a wise old bee,
'Just trust your wings, forget the spree!'
Yet nectar's sweet, it calls them back,
They whir through petals, never lack.

A flower yawns, gives a big sigh,
'Why do you zoom and never try?
Relax, dear friends, soak up the sun,
Less fussing means more nectar fun!'

With laughter echoing from above,
They zip and swirl, like sips of love.
In the bloom-burst glow, joy ignites,
As they flit away into the nights.

The Bonfire Chronicles

The flames danced high, sparks taking flight,
While crabs in tuxedos waltzed with delight.
The marshmallows winked from their sticky perch,
As the ocean laughed at the evening's lurch.

A coconut rolled, joining the fun,
It slipped on the sand, oh what a run!
With each little mishap, the giggles grew loud,
As the moon took a bow to the gathering crowd.

Fish in the icebox, a boisterous crew,
Wishing for freedom, to join in the view.
But they'd just flop and flop, a soggy ballet,
Leaving us all in fits of display.

By dawn, we were tired, yet smiles were so wide,
As we forged lasting bonds on this tropical ride.
The lessons of laughter nestled in our hearts,
As the morning sun broke, fresh mischief departs.

Nestled Between the Tropics

A parrot squawked out sweet gossip each day,
While iguanas basked, come what may.
The palm trees swayed, whispering tales,
Of tourists caught in hilarious fails.

With flip-flops that flip and hats that flew,
And sunburns unwelcome in shades of bright hue.
The beach balls exploded, a colorful sight,
While laughter erupted like waves in the night.

The lifeguard dozed, dreaming of gold,
While his sunblock adventures quietly unfolded.
Miguel rolled in, with ice cream galore,
But tripped on a towel, ending up on the floor.

Yet through all the chaos and giggling spree,
We knew those moments were wild and free.
Tucked between laughter, we found our reprise,
As the sun set it all with a tropical sigh.

Legends Woven in Sea Glass

Sea glass legends whisper with glee,
Of mermaids who jig and tumble by sea.
A crab in a crown had plans to rule,
But slipped on a shell—oh, the beach was a pool!

Old boats with stories bobbed by the shore,
While starfish giggled and begged for encore.
The waves told of pirates with terrible rhymes,
Whose treasure was laughter, a mystery of times.

Children with buckets gathered their loot,
Collecting the stories, both funny and cute.
The ocean winked secrets to the sand,
As gulls tried to steal each scoop from their hand.

With every find, a new joke would spin,
About mermaids dancing and where they had been.
So if you wander and hear the waves clash,
Know the legends are made of soft, glittery sea glass.

The Color of Mango Skies

The sun kissed the horizon, what a sight!
Mango skies told jokes, soft and bright.
The breeze held a giggle, so light in the air,
While bananas in pajamas danced without care.

Laughter blended with the scent of sweet fruits,
As pineapples showed off in their fancy boots.
A sloth on a tree had a splendid retreat,
Gliding down slowly, what a hilarious feat!

With ice-cold drinks served in coconut crowns,
We toasted to moments where laughter abounds.
And as the stars sprinkled the evening with cheer,
The mango skies laughed, "Bring more friends here!"

Under the canopy, shared stories took flight,
Of mishaps and wonders that spark joy each night.
In the land where the sunset steals every sigh,
We danced in the colors of the mango sky.

The Embrace of Exotic Flora

In a garden where the flowers dance,
A parrot jokes, it takes a chance.
With colors bright, it starts to sing,
A tune that makes the blossoms swing.

The orchids whisper, 'Is that a bee?'
'Nah, just a butterfly, sipping tea!'
They giggle softly in the sun,
As lizards race—a lively run.

A cactus tried to tell a tale,
But ended up with prickly mail.
The roses laughed in fragrant glee,
As ants marched by, a grand parade spree.

Essence of the Emerald Waters

In waters deep, the fish do prance,
A turtle joins, no need to dance.
With fins that flop, and bubbles blown,
They share a joke, as currents moan.

The frogs in chorus, voices loud,
Croak out their secrets, very proud.
While raindrops laugh upon the leaves,
A splash—a frog jumps, what a tease!

A crab wears shades, a real cool cat,
While snails roll by, all slow and fat.
In a splash of green, the fun won't cease,
For every wave brings joy and peace.

Elysian Echoes of the Rainforest

Beneath the canopy, the monkeys swing,
They share a laugh, a cheeky thing.
With vines as ropes and leaves as capes,
They chatter stories, making shapes.

A sloth drags slow, with perfect grace,
Responding late to every race.
With each slow blink, the forest sighs,
While toucans giggle, painting skies.

A jaguar naps beneath the trees,
Dreaming of fish and buzzing bees.
His snores echo, a rhythmic beat,
As nature dances, life is sweet.

Mosaics of Tropical Wildlife

In patches bright, the creatures play,
A capybara finds a way.
With friends that laugh all through the day,
They frolic in their own ballet.

A flamingo trips on one fine leg,
And falls right in, a funny beg.
The crowd erupts, they're in a spin,
A dance-off in the mud to win.

The monkeys boast of silly tricks,
While iguanas do their flicks.
They blend their colors, bright and bold,
In nature's art, a story told.

Reveries in Twilight Hues

Under the blush of evening's glow,
Crabs in tuxedos steal the show.
They boogie down on sandy feet,
Sharing secrets with the heat.

The gulls hold court on ocean's crest,
While fish play chess; they are the best.
A mermaid laughs, her hair a swirl,
As barnacles join in with a twirl.

The sun dips low, a shy old friend,
As coconuts roll, hoping to blend.
The stars peek out, all the while,
A narwhal's joke makes the night smile.

In twilight's sketch, all creatures play,
With laughter echoing far away.
Adventures bloom with every tide,
In a world where jests collide.

Castaway Melodies on the Shore

Lost on shores with a bumbling breeze,
A toucan croons between the trees.
He strums a tune on a coconut drum,
While sunbathing lizards hum along, dumb.

Shells gossip as the waves conspire,
Mermaids joking with a water flyer.
Sand's fine dust forms a fanciful dance,
As crabs prance forth in a funny trance.

A shipwrecked mate with an eye patch bold,
Looks for treasure, but finds fish untold.
Coconuts roll and crash in laughter,
While seashells gossip of what comes after.

In harmony with the ocean's heart,
Nature's concert is a wondrous art.
Beneath the sun, all worries fade,
In this seaside serenade.

The Poetry of the Palmetto Skies

Palmettos sway with a rhythmic cheer,
As iguanas hold a funny career.
With shades to shield their scaly eyes,
They ponder life, oh what a surprise!

A chubby parrot with a flair for rhyme,
Chats with the breeze about the time.
He wishes for more snacks and fun,
While dreaming of a tropical run.

Under the prints of silly feet,
Raccoons toast to their next treat.
Bats hang down in a comical spree,
Reading tales from a palm tree of glee.

As daydreams float through that sky so wide,
Nutty wonder lives alongside pride.
Amidst the laughter, stories bloom,
In a world filled with fun, never gloom.

Dances of the Daring Dolphins

Dolphins leaping with joyous flair,
Their cuts and spins draw folks from near.
With each splash, a story unfolds,
As schools of fish grin at their bolds.

A walrus winks with a seaweed hat,
Giggling away on a lounging mat.
Crabs take stage for a surprise show,
While jellyfish flaunt their neon glow.

The catches of the day make a mess,
As dolphins chirp, 'We love this excess!'
Balancing balls with tails so sleek,
Their comic antics leave us weak.

Among the ocean's frothy delight,
All creatures join this joy-filled rite.
In every splash, they find their bliss,
Casting waves of laughter—a joyous kiss.

Adrift in Aquatic Dreams

In a boat so small, it's barely afloat,
I met a fish wearing a tiny coat.
He offered me snacks, like seaweed chips,
But frowned when I said, "I prefer dips!"

We drifted along, sharing silly tales,
Of crabs in sunglasses and giddy snails.
The waves giggled back, making big splashes,
While mermaids fought over seashells and splashes.

A dolphin danced close, wearing bright shades,
Juggling sea cucumbers, he never fades.
With laughter afloat, like bubbles we gleamed,
In a sea of dreams, where nothing is deemed.

So if you see us, just wave and smile,
We're cruising the currents, living in style.
For humor's the anchor in this wild sea,
As we sail through life, just fish and me.

Colors of the Coral Carnival

A flamingo in feathers, all colors combined,
Painted polka dots, oh what a find!
He tiptoes through reefs, a dance so absurd,
While seahorses giggle, they hardly deterred.

An octopus juggles with colorful balls,
While fish in tuxedos ride on coral walls.
The clownfish keeps cracking the same silly joke,
Every bubble it forms erupts into smoke.

Underwater parades with shells all aglow,
Crabs in a conga line, moving slow.
Mermaids trade glitter for tacos from rays,
In this carnival whirl, we laugh through the days.

So join in the fun, bring your best dance moves,
Amidst all the ocean's ludicrous grooves.
In colors of laughter, let's share our delight,
In the carnival's essence, everything feels right.

The Spirit of Silken Sands

On shores of gold with pillows of sun,
A crab dressed in boots thought he'd have fun.
He strutted and danced, like he owned the beach,
While all of us marveled, oh what a peach!

The seagulls were spectating, popcorn in hand,
As the crab made a scene, drawing quite the band.
With a tap and a shuffle, he stole the show,
While sandcastles crumbled, their reign at a low.

A turtle took selfies, and giggled aloud,
With seaweed wigs, he felt really proud.
The sun winked down, painted all in hues,
As laughter and sand blended joyful views.

So here on the sands, where silliness reigns,
With boots and with selfies, nothing remains.
Join all the festivities, don't be so bland,
Just dive into laughter, where tales expand.

Profiles of the Pristine Shore

A beach ball stole the scene, rolled with great glee,
Chasing children around, like folks at a spree.
With giggles and splashes, the fun never ends,
As sea turtles winked at their carefree friends.

The sand's a big canvas, where toes leave a mark,
Portraits of joy, painted bright in the park.
"Who made this?" they wonder, "It's wild and it's grand!"

While surfboards stand guard like a loyal band.

Seashells in colors of every delight,
Each whispers secrets, in moon's silver light.
With laughter like thunder and joy in their hearts,
The ocean keeps giving its playful smarts.

So join in the madness, take a seat by the shore,
Where funny is fashion and laughter's a chore.
In the profiles of moments, we always will share,
The joy of these shores, free of every care.

Pebbles of Wisdom on the Beach

On sandy shores where seagulls play,
A crab told jokes to brighten the day.
He pinched his friend in a silly brawl,
Said, "It's just a pinch, don't take it all!"

Footprints dance under the sun's warm light,
A starfish whispered, "Don't lose your bite!"
With shells as hats, the clams had a feast,
Laughing at waves, they were never the least.

The sun took a dip, the tides made a show,
As dolphins leaped high, putting on a flow.
With every splash, they made little waves,
Their giggles echoed, oh how the beach braves!

When nightfall came and stars took their place,
The crabs shared tales in a cozy embrace.
On pebbles of wisdom, they shared hearty lore,
With laughter and joy, they asked for more!

Whimsies of the Waterfall

At the base of the falls with splashes so bright,
A frog wore a crown, feeling quite light.
"Ribbit, dear fish! Come share a grand tale,
Of dancing in bubbles or riding a whale!"

The tigers swung in the trees overhead,
A sloth made up stories, all fur and dread.
"Why run when you can hang out and chill?
I'll snack on these leaves, I've got time to kill!"

Octopus held court in a swirling parade,
"Who brings the snacks? It's a new escapade!"
With colors so bright, sea urchins took stand,
They all joined the fun, it was simply grand.

As rainbows arched high, they danced off the rocks,
With waterfalls singing combining their knocks.
In splashes of laughter, joy flowed anew,
The whimsies abounded, and all of them grew!

Tales of the Tropical Breeze

The breeze tiptoed in through wide-open doors,
Whispering secrets of faraway shores.
"Hey, sunshine! Got all day to spark,
Let's chase the butterflies till it's dark!"

Palm fronds flapped like excited old fans,
Swaying and giggling, they joined in the plans.
"Watch out for the monkey with bananas to spare,
He'll challenge you first; watch out for the flair!"

The parrot squawked loud with a vibrant delight,
"Who needs a stage? I can fly, what a sight!"
In circles they spun, their laughter like chimes,
They made up new rhythms, syncopated rhymes.

As day turned to dusk with stars shining bright,
The breezy shenanigans danced into night.
With every soft gust, a chuckle would roll,
The tropical zest filled the heart and the soul!

Voices from the Verdant Canopy

In the jungle's heart, where the parrots sing,
Monkeys spun tales of their wild fling.
"Last week," said one, with a glimmering eye,
"I wore a flower crown and danced on high!"

Lemurs played tag among vines with delight,
While sloths cheered on from their branches so tight.
"Race us!" they hollered, but no one would move,
Time is a luxury in the sloth's groove.

Through laughter and chatter, wise wisdom arose,
From an ancient tree that glittered with prose.
"Life's a grand party; don't forget to play!
Join the ruckus and brighten your day!"

As dusk settled down with a magical hue,
The jungle erupted in fun, and they flew.
Voices echoed sweet from the canopy high,
With giggles and joy that reached for the sky!

Reflections in Tropical Rain

Raindrops dance on my head,
Umbrellas flip, so much fun!
A monkey steals my snack right away,
Laughing hard, we're on the run.

Splashing puddles, shoes all wet,
Fish swim by, without a care,
A parrot squawks, 'What a mess!'
I just giggle, life's quite rare.

Sun breaks through, what a sight,
Rainbow arcs through trees so green,
We stumble, we trip, but it's alright,
In this chaos, joy is seen.

Next day shines, it starts to rain,
Round and round, we play our game,
Tropical storms can't dim our glee,
Every drop, a laugh, a claim.

Murmurs of the Mystic Lagoon

Waves tease me, they splash my toes,
A crab scuttles, as fast as a bolt,
Frogs serenade with ribbiting prose,
Mermaids laugh at the joke they cult.

Nights filled with fireflies' bright glow,
The turtles dance with glee, oh what fun!
An old fish claims he's younger, though,
I just chuckle, he's been outdone.

Mystic waters, so cool and clear,
A treasure hunt for shells begins,
Yet all we find is some old gear,
But laughter beats all, that's our win!

Under stars, stories take flight,
We share tales of troubles past,
In the lagoon's serene, funny light,
We'll keep laughing, this joy will last.

Journeys through Jungle Canopies

Swinging vines, oh what a sight,
Monkeys chase as we climb high,
Parrots giggle at our fright,
A lizard mocks, oh my, oh my!

Mossy paths, we dance and trip,
Swaying branches serve our quest,
A toucan lands, cute beak and lip,
With goofy smiles, we've been blessed.

Sudden rains turn trails to slips,
Up we go, down we slide,
With every trip, we laugh, not gripe,
In sticky heat, we take the ride.

At journey's end, on a log we rest,
With tales of the clumsiness we birthed,
In the jungle's heart, we feel so blessed,
For in this mishap, pure joy is unearthed.

Fragments of Forgotten Islands

Casting nets, we hope for fish,
But socks come up, oh what a stash!
A broken boat, a quirky wish,
Each wave's punchline is a splash.

Palm trees sway with a chuckle light,
As waves recite their rhymes so bold,
Old maps lead us not far, but right,
To pirate tales that never get old.

Barefoot strolling on sandy shores,
We dig for treasures, find a shoe,
Starfish grin as seagulls roar,
Yelling, 'Ha, what's wrong with you?'

Evenings glow with coconut drinks,
We toast to rocks that chant our name,
In the heart of laughter, no one thinks,
This island's charm is our claim to fame.

Odyssey of Fragrant Flora

In a land where the pineapples play,
Coconuts dance in a breezy ballet.
Papayas giggle, the mangoes hum,
While the limes in robes invite everyone.

A toucan tried to juggle some grapes,
But missed and fell, in hilarious shapes.
The orchids winking, with petals so bright,
Said, "Join our party; it's quite a sight!"

With every sip of the coconut milk,
Laughter rises, as smooth as silk.
The parrots squawking their favorite jokes,
Filling the air with the sound of folks.

Under the palms with shadows that sway,
We dance and feast till the close of day.
In this fragrant wonder, all cares fade,
With amusing chaos, life's grand parade.

Enigma of the Endless Horizon

Beneath the sun on a banana boat,
A crab in shades takes a funny float.
He waved to a fish, who winked in reply,
While seagulls competed to snag the sky.

A dolphin in flip-flops came for the fun,
Juggling some shells, oh what a run!
With splashes of laughter that filled the blue,
The ocean's secrets were giggled anew.

The sun painted skies in vibrant hues,
As turtles played cards with some colorful clues.
They pondered mysteries of the soft sand,
Chatting in riddles, oh so unplanned.

As the horizon stretched far and wide,
The laughter mixed with the ocean tide.
With a wink to the stars, we bid adieu,
In this endless realm where the silly grew.

The Art of the Tropical Sunset

At twilight, the sky wore a vibrant grin,
While crickets chirped a melodious din.
A squirrel in sunglasses held court on a tree,
Declaring, "This sunset's the best, can't you see?"

A beehive choir joined in to sing,
While the fireflies danced, their tiny bling.
The sun dipped low, a grand show indeed,
As shadows stretched out, like a painter's creed.

Coconuts swapped tales of the day's delight,
While rubbery lizards got ready for night.
They laughed at their antics, flippant and spry,
As the stars peeked out, low in the sky.

With a splash of pink and a splash of gold,
These moments of joy were pure treasure to hold.
In this whimsical world where antics abound,
The art of sunset brings laughter around.

Beneath the Tropic Stars

Underneath the twinkling lights,
The iguana danced with all his might.
A parrot laughed, a coconut fell,
As crabs held court, oh what a swell!

Stars above, like scattered sweets,
The monkey jived, missed a beat.
To charm the skies, he'd take a chance,
But tumbled down, no second glance!

Vignettes of Vibrant Flora

A flower flaunted, bold and bright,
Claimed it could start a rainbow fight.
The bees buzzed loud, in playful dread,
While petals giggled, "Let's turn red!"

A cactus moaned, "I need a buddy!"
The daisies whispered, "That's too muddy!"
With all their shades, they laughed and spun,
In sunny plots, oh what fun begun!

Legends of the Lush Waters

A fish named Fred with big, wide eyes,
Swam through tales that made him wise.
He found a shoe, thought it a boat,
Sailed the tide with a silly float.

A turtle hummed, "I'll race you there!"
But snoozed instead in sun-kissed air.
The crabs held bets with silly cheers,
While dolphins cracked jokes, no room for fears!

Chronicles of Coastal Echoes

Along the shore, the seagulls squawked,
As beach balls flew, the children talked.
A sandcastle grand faced waves with pride,
But tumbled down - oh what a ride!

Nearby, a crab wore shades so cool,
Promised to teach the tidepool school.
"Join me pals!" he called with glee,
As waves crashed down, oh slippery spree!

Chronicles of the Tidal Wave

A wave came crashing, oh what a sight,
It grabbed my hat and took off in flight.
I chased behind, my flip-flops flew,
While seagulls cackled, 'What's wrong with you?'

My drink took a dive, a splash on the shore,
The beach ball giggled, then rolled out for more.
A crab waved hello, he just couldn't care,
As my picnic lunch floated off in the air.

A toddler laughed loud, pointing my way,
As I stumbled and slipped, no grace in my sway.
The tide pulled my towel, my sandwich it took,
Such is the life in this beachy nook.

Yet with each wave I can't help but cheer,
For oddball events bring my friends a great cheer.
In this sandy paradise, with giggles so bright,
We dance with the tide, till the fall of the night.

The Aroma of Spiced Memories

In a kitchen so bright, spices twirl and whirl,
Garlic and ginger a fragrant swirl.
My uncle danced in, a chef filled with zest,
Stirring the pot, hoping for the best.

"With a pinch of this, and a dash of that,
You'll turn out a feast, or at least a nice chat!"
But as he sneezed, it sent spices afloat,
Now everyone's laughing—just look at that coat!

Chili went flying, a red spicy cloud,
The cat ran for cover, so clever and proud.
While I tried to catch it, I slipped on a peel,
Now the kitchen's a circus, that's quite a meal!

But at the dinner, we chuckle and sigh,
As we feast on our mess, oh my, oh my!
With memories steeped in flavors so bold,
Our laughter fills up the stories retold.

Laughter Under Coconut Palms

Beneath the tall palms where the coconuts sway,
A parrot squawks jokes in a colorful way.
He roams the green branches, a comical sight,
Making us giggle from morning till night.

A monkey swung by, wearing socks on his paws,
With a slip and a slide, he forgot his own laws.
While a turtle sang tunes, oh so off-key,
Just add some more laughter, and that's fine by me!

We played beach volleyball, with laughter so loud,
Ball ended up stuck in a coconut crowd.
As surges of giggles envelop the scene,
It's hard not to grin in this life's sunny sheen.

At last as the sun dips, we sit side by side,
With stories and chuckles that swell up with pride.
These memories bright, they'll never grow dim,
In the fun of the tropics, we're all in on the whim.

The Painter's Palette of Sunset

A painter stood up on the edge of the bay,
With colors so wild, splashed everywhere play.
With yellows and pinks, he danced with each stroke,
Till a breeze came along and it jiggled—then soaked!

"Oh no," he exclaimed as the canvas took flight,
His masterpiece soaring into the night.
A fish jumped up high, stole the brush with a splash,
Then back in the water, a bold underwater dash!

The crowd burst in laughter at this funny sight,
As the painter gave chase, wiping tears of delight.
With a flick and a swirl, he inked the great fowl,
What fun to create in the hues of the howl!

Now the sunset is painted in giggles and gleam,
With splashes of color, like a dreamer's sweet dream.
No canvas too messy, no hues that won't blend,
In laughter and joy, we create and transcend.

www.ingramcontent.com/pod-product-compliance
Lightning Source LLC
Chambersburg PA
CBHW072220070526
44585CB00015B/1423